MIDWEEK HUMOR

IRENE XANDERENA

ISBN: 979-8-8691-6849-8

Published by
Eyereneeswords
Email: life@eyereneeswords.com
Website: www.eyereneeswords.com

CONTENT

Acknowledgment   v

Introduction   vii

Preface   ix

Midweek Humor   13

10 Ways to Get Through the Work Week   105

10 Reasons for a Monday to Friday
Work Week   107

ACKNOWLEDGMENT

First and foremost, I want to thank all the Wednesday warriors out there for inspiring this book. Your ability to keep a smile on your face despite the mid-week madness is truly commendable.

I also want to express my gratitude to my family and friends for putting up with my constant puns and jokes during the writing process–you guys are the real MVP's of laughter.

And lastly, a big shoutout to the coffee industry for fueling my late-night writing sessions and providing the much-needed caffeine boost to survive those hump days. Cheers!

I would like to extend my heartfelt appreciation to all those who find humor in the middle of the week and dare to embrace the absurdity and lightheartedness it brings. Your support and laughter have made this book possible, and I hope it brings a smile to your face as much as it did to mine while writing it.

INTRODUCTION

I started writing the humor series in 2023. Humans tend to approach life and their careers with great seriousness. But once they grasp the concept that life is akin to a game, they will find it more pleasurable.

Why did I write a humor book about midweek, you ask? Well, picture this: it's Tuesday, you're halfway through the workweek, and you're desperately trying to convince yourself that Friday is just around the corner. But let's be honest, we all know Wednesday is that obnoxious speed bump that ruins the flow.

So, I wrote this book to provide a much-needed comedic escape from the mid-week madness. Think of it as your personal survival guide to navigate the treacherous terrain of Wednesdays, one chuckle at a time. And hey, if it can make you forget about the pile of unfinished reports on your desk for a few minutes, I consider that a job well done!

PREFACE

"Believe you can and you're halfway there!"
Theodore Roosevelt [1858-1919]

Ever found yourself sitting at your desk on a Wednesday, contemplating the meaning of life while your coffee grows cold, and your to-do list grows longer? Well, fear not, my fellow sufferers of mid-week madness, for I have written a humor book dedicated to the absurdity of those hump day blues.

Whether you need a laugh, a distraction, or just an excuse to procrastinate, this book is the perfect companion to survive the midweek mayhem with a smile on your face and a snort of laughter that'll surely confuse your coworkers. Midweek, that notorious hump day, often leaves us feeling drained and in desperate need of a pick-me-up. It is during these moments of monotony that I found solace in humor, using it as a coping mechanism to inject some much-needed laughter into the mundane routine.

With this book, I aim to share that joy and provide a humorous escape from the midweek blues, reminding readers to embrace the absurdity and find joy even in the most ordinary of days. Amid the daily grind, the midweek slump can feel like a never-ending struggle. It's the point where motivation wanes, and the weekend seems too far away. That's why I embarked on the journey of writing a humor book about midweek – to inject some much-needed laughter and levity into those seemingly endless days, reminding readers that humor can be found even in the most mundane moments.

Mondays are too early to be funny; Fridays are too busy being everyone's favorite, and poor Wednesday is just stuck in the middle, longing for some comedic love. I mean, have you ever seen a mid-week meme that didn't make you giggle? Me neither! So, I decided to dedicate an entire book to celebrating the unsung hero of the workweek– Wednesday, the day that's both close enough to the weekend to dream and far enough from Monday to rejoice.

Get ready for a wild ride filled with laughter, because midweek madness is about to get a hilarious twist! Wednesday is just sitting there, smirking at you, like the mischievous middle child of the workweek. Get ready to laugh your midweek blues away and join me on this hilarious journey through the wild world of Wednesdays.

Trust me, after reading this book, you'll never underestimate the power of a Wednesday again! Wednesdays are secretly the funniest day of the week! Think about it, Monday gets all the hate, Friday gets all the hype, but Wednesday? It's just there, hanging out like the class clown in a quiet classroom. Now I invite you to join me on the Midweek humor journey.

MIDWEEK HUMOR

1

What do you call a
Wednesday that feels like
a Friday?

Wishful thinking!

2

How do you make Wednesday more bearable?

You can't!

3

Midweek is like the middle child of the week, often overlooked and underappreciated.

4

Midweek is that hump
day where you're both
relieved that the weekend
is approaching, yet
still drowning in the
responsibilities of the week.

5

Midweek is like that awkward moment when you realize you're halfway through a Zoom meeting and still in your pajamas.

6

Midweek is the pivotal point where you're simultaneously relieved it's not Monday anymore but also desperately longing for Friday to arrive.

7

Midweek is the time when you start questioning your life choices and wonder if becoming a professional napper is a viable career option.

8

What's the difference between a calendar and midweek?

A calendar has dates, but midweek has "Why me"?

9

What did one wall say to the
other midweek?

I'll meet you at the corner!

10

Why don't scientists trust atoms midweek?

Because they make up everything!

11

What did the grape say to the banana midweek?

"Stop peeling so much pressure!"

12

Why did the tomato turn
red midweek?

Because it saw the
salad dressing!

13

Why don't skeletons fight midweek?

They don't have the guts!

14

Midweek is like a rollercoaster ride - you're halfway through the week, holding on tight, and praying for the weekend to arrive!

15

Midweek is that awkward stage where you've already forgotten what happened on Monday, but Friday still feels light-years away.

16

Midweek is like a bad hair day for your soul - it's just a little bit off and you can't wait for it to be over.

17

Midweek is when you realize you've been wearing your shirt inside out all day, but you're too tired to care because coffee hasn't kicked in yet.

18

Midweek is that magical
time when you start
having a conversation with
your plant, and it seems
completely normal.

19

Midweek is when you start considering changing your name to "Friday" just to make it feel closer.

20

Midweek is like a long-forgotten TV show - you vaguely remember it exists, but you're not sure if you actually want to watch it.

21

Midweek is when you start negotiating with yourself about how many more days you can get away with wearing the same pair of pants before doing laundry.

22

Midweek is like a sneaky ninja - it creeps up on you, steals your energy, and disappears before you even notice.

23

Midweek is like a midlife crisis for the workweek - it's not quite as young and exciting like Monday, but it's not as well-deserved as Friday either.

24

Midweek is when you start questioning your sanity and consider running away to join the circus because surely being a clown is less stressful than your job.

25

Midweek is like a stale doughnut - it's not fresh and exciting like Monday, but it's not quite as disappointing as realizing it's only Wednesday.

26

Midweek is like a never-ending traffic jam in your brain - thoughts are stuck, motivation is nowhere to be found, and all you want is a teleportation device to Friday.

27

Midweek is when you start fantasizing about winning the lottery and quitting your job to become a professional vacationer, but then reality hits and you remember you didn't even buy a ticket.

28

Midweek is like a cruel joke
- you're halfway through the
week, but it feels like you've
been stuck in a time loop
for eternity.

29

Midweek is when you find yourself having full conversations with your office coffee maker and considering it your new best friend because human interaction is overrated.

30

Midweek is like a messy hair day for your schedule - you've lost track of time, missed meetings, and now you're just desperately hoping no one notices.

31

What did the coffee say to the tea on Wednesday?

"We're halfway there let's keep brewing!"

32

What did the calendar say to
Wednesday?

"You're just a hump day, but
I've got a whole month to
deal with!"

33

Why did the tomato turn red on Wednesday?

It saw the weekend approaching and blushed with excitement.

34

What did Wednesday say to the other days of the week?

"I'm the middle child, always overlooked, but I'm still important!"

35

What did the math book say to Wednesday?

"I'm filled with problems, but at least we're halfway through solving them!"

36

Why did the clock feel relieved on Wednesday?

It finally had a midweek break from all the ticking and tocking.

37

Why did the chicken cross
the road on Wednesday?

To remind everyone that
there's still work to be done
before the weekend.

38

What do you call a
Wednesday that feels like
a Monday?

A "womp day" - it's the worst
of both worlds!

39

Why did the pencil feel rebellious on Wednesday?

It started drawing outside the lines, embracing its midweek creativity.

40

What did the light bulb say to Wednesday?

"You're the bright spot in the middle of the week, keep shining!"

41

What did Wednesday say to
the coffee mug?

"Fill me up, I need all the
caffeine to get through the
rest of the week!"

42

Why did the chef make extra
soup on Wednesday?

It's the perfect midweek
comfort food, warming the
soul until Friday.

43

Why did the office printer refuse to cooperate on Wednesday?

It was experiencing a midweek paper jam and needed a siesta.

44

Midweek is the awkward
middle child of the week, not
as exciting as the beginning
or as satisfying as the end.

45

If Midweek had a theme song, it would be "I Will Survive" by Gloria Gaynor because it takes true resilience to get through it.

46

Midweek is like a long-
distance relationship with
the weekend - you're so close,
yet so far away.

47

Midweek is like the feeling of finding an empty fridge when you're craving a midnight snack - disappointing and a little bit sad.

48

Midweek is the time when you realize you have more tabs open in your mind than on your computer.

49

Midweek is when you contemplate creating a time machine just to fast forward to Friday.

50

Midweek is when your motivation takes a vacation and leaves you stranded in a desert of responsibilities.

51

Midweek is like a marathon, except instead of miles, you count the number of yawns you let out during meetings.

52

Midweek is when the struggle to 'adult' is at its peak, and you secretly wish you could trade places with a carefree squirrel.

53

Midweek is where dreams go to hibernate until the weekend wakes them up with a jolt of caffeine.

54

Midweek is like a reality
TV show where you're
the star, trying to balance
work, life, and the constant
desire to nap.

55

Midweek is when you start questioning the existence of time because it feels like it's moving slower than a snail on tranquilizers.

56

Midweek is like a traffic jam of deadlines, meetings, and unanswered emails, leaving you stuck in a never-ending cycle of chaos.

57

Midweek is when you contemplate starting a petition to make Wednesdays optional because who really needs them anyway?

58

Midweek is like a puzzle with missing pieces - you're trying to put it all together, but something feels off.

59

Midweek is when you start daydreaming about being on a tropical island, sipping margaritas instead of sitting in a stuffy office.

60

Midweek is like a game of hide-and-seek, except you're seeking the motivation to get through the rest of the week, and it's hiding somewhere in a parallel universe.

61

What do you call a Wednesday that feels like a Monday?

A "Monnesday"!

62

What did one Wednesday say to the other?

"Is it Friday yet? I'm losing track of time!"

63

Why did the calendar refuse to go to work on Wednesday?

Because it wanted to have a midweekend!

64

Why did the skeleton go to
the party on Wednesday?

Because it had a bone to pick
with the week!

65

How do you keep a
Wednesday from
feeling lonely?

Invite "Hump Day" for
a playdate!

66

Why did the coffee file a police report on Wednesday?

It got mugged!

67

What did Wednesday say to the weekend?

"Don't worry, I'll keep the weekdays under control!"

68

What did one Wednesday say to the other when they were feeling down? "Chin up, the weekend is just a few days away!"

69

Why did the computer go to therapy on Wednesday?

It had a case of "midweek glitches"!

70

Why did the pencil feel anxious on Wednesday?

It couldn't decide if it should lead or be erased!

71

How does a Wednesday feel after a good workout?

Revulsive and fabulous!

72

What's Wednesday's favorite type of humor?

"Wacky Wednesday" jokes, of course!

73

Midweek is like that awkward stage where you're too far from Monday to be motivated and too far from Friday to be excited.

74

Midweek is like a reality check, reminding you that you're not a superhero and that you actually need sleep and caffeine to function.

75

Midweek is when you realize that you've already worn your favorite outfit twice this week and now have to resort to the back of the closet.

76

Midweek is like a puzzle, you're not quite sure how all the pieces fit together, but you're determined to make it work.

77

Midweek is when you start contemplating a career as a professional procrastinator because you've become an expert at avoiding tasks.

78

Midweek is like a comedy show, you're constantly trying to find the humor in the chaos of work!

79

Why did the pencil feel anxious on Wednesdays?

It couldn't handle the pressure of being halfway through the week.

80

Why did the calendar get into a fight with Wednesday?

Because it wanted to skip straight to the weekend and Wednesday wasn't having any of it.

81

Why did Wednesday break up with Monday and Tuesday?

It wanted to have a midweek fling with Friday!

82

Why did Wednesday go to therapy?

It was tired of being stuck in the middle and needed help coping with this condition.

83

Why did Wednesday bring
an umbrella to work?

It wanted to stay dry in
case of midweek showers
of boredom!

84

What did Wednesday say to Thursday?

"I don't like you! You and Friday are BFFs, Monday and Tuesday are BFFs, and you all gossip about me!

85

Why did Wednesday feel like a superhero?

Because it had the power to make the weekend feel closer.

86

How did Wednesday react
when it found out it was
Wednesday again?

It exclaimed, "Oh my days, it's
me again! Hump day!

87

On Wednesdays, I like to pretend I'm a sloth, moving at a leisurely pace since I'm neither Monday (energy-draining) nor Friday (tantalizing proximity to the weekend).

88

What do you call a Wednesday that feels like a Friday?

A midweek miracle!

89

Why did the calendar refuse to go on a date with Wednesday?

It said, "Sorry, I'm booked!"

90

How do you keep
Wednesday motivated?

Remind it that it's only
two days away from
the weekend!

104

10 WAYS TO GET THROUGH THE WORK WEEK

1. **Prioritize tasks:** Determine the most important tasks and focus on completing them first.

2. **Break it down:** Divide larger tasks into smaller, manageable chunks to avoid feeling overwhelmed.

3. **Time management:** Create a schedule or to-do list to allocate specific time slots for different tasks.

4. **Avoid multitasking:** Instead, focus on one task at a time to maintain productivity and efficiency.

5. **Delegate when possible:** If you have the opportunity, delegate some tasks to trusted colleagues or team members.

6. **Take breaks:** Schedule short breaks throughout the day to rest and recharge, which can boost productivity and reduce stress.

7. **Practice self-care:** Prioritize self-care activities like exercise, healthy eating, and getting enough sleep to maintain energy levels.

8. **Avoid unnecessary distractions:** Minimize interruptions such as social media notifications or non-essential meetings.

9. **Stay organized:** Keep your workspace tidy and organized to minimize time wasted searching for documents or supplies.

10. **Seek support:** Reach out to colleagues, friends, or family for emotional support or assistance with workload if needed.

10 REASONS FOR A MONDAY TO FRIDAY WORK WEEK

1. **Tradition:** The Monday through Friday workweek has been established as a societal norm and has been followed for decades.

2. **Consistency:** Having a consistent work schedule helps individuals plan their personal lives and maintain a healthy work-life balance.

3. **Alignment with other businesses:** Many businesses and organizations operate Monday through Friday, enabling smoother collaboration and communication.

4. **Economic efficiency:** The Monday through Friday workweek aligns with the majority of businesses operating hours, maximizing productivity and efficiency.

5. **Work-life balance:** The standard workweek allows individuals to have their weekends off, providing time to relax, spend with family, and pursue personal interests.

6. **Cultural and social expectations:** Society has conditioned us to view Monday through Friday as the typical work schedule, making it easier to align with societal norms and expectations.

7. **Access to services:** With most businesses operating during the same workweek, individuals have easier access to services they may need, such as banking, healthcare, or government services.

8. **School and education:** The Monday through Friday workweek aligns with school schedules, allowing parents to be available for their children's education and extracurricular activities.

9. **Travel and leisure:** The standard workweek leaves the weekends free for travel, vacations, and leisure activities, as many tourist destinations and recreational facilities are busiest on weekends.

10. **Psychological benefits:** Having a consistent routine and knowing when to expect work and when to expect time off can provide a sense of stability and reduce stress and anxiety.